Everyday Focus is a wonderful collection of poems written with love about family and everyday experiences. I found it to be very thought provoking and inspirational and believe anyone who loves poetry will enjoy reading it over and over.

—Jerry Stephenson

I highly recommend reading Patricka Daley-Pledger's free style poetry, *Everyday Focus*. She touches on different aspects of life that everyone can relate to—you will chuckle, cry, or laugh out loud. It is timeless—one you would keep.

—Christiana J. Bridgewater
Attorney and Certified Public Accountant
Queens, New York

everyday FOCUS

PATRICKA DALEY-PLEDGER

everyday FOCUS

A COLLECTION *of* POEMS

TATE PUBLISHING *& Enterprises*

Everyday Focus
Copyright © 2011 by Patricka Daley-Pledger. All rights reserved.

No part of this publication may be reproduced, stored in a retrieval system or transmitted in any way by any means, electronic, mechanical, photocopy, recording or otherwise without the prior permission of the author except as provided by USA copyright law.

The opinions expressed by the author are not necessarily those of Tate Publishing, LLC.

Published by Tate Publishing & Enterprises, LLC
127 E. Trade Center Terrace | Mustang, Oklahoma 73064 USA
1.888.361.9473 | www.tatepublishing.com

Tate Publishing is committed to excellence in the publishing industry. The company reflects the philosophy established by the founders, based on Psalm 68:11,
"The Lord gave the word and great was the company of those who published it."

Book design copyright © 2011 by Tate Publishing, LLC. All rights reserved.
Cover design by Kellie Vincent
Interior design by Sarah Kirchen

Published in the United States of America

ISBN:978-1-61346-047-4
Poetry / Inspirational & Religious
11.10.24

Acknowledgments

I am profoundly grateful for the enthusiastic
support from my work - family:

*Sheila Sherlock, Ellen Segal, Kira Ferebee,
Laura Sibley* and the rest of the crew,
too many to mention.

I would never be able to continue life on such
a positive road, of what would otherwise be a
difficult bereavement period,
if it wasn't for the caring nature of

Robin Odom, Clover Collins Anthony,
and *Carrie Pender.*

They knew just when I needed a sisterly hug,
flowers and a loving pup from the shelter.

I could never take for granted the
wholehearted support of
my friends in New York:

Dawn Barton, Alvin Barnett
and *Althea McLeod.*

More love to you, my siblings:

Loxley, Paulette, Louis, Jacqueline and *Suzet,*

Loving daughter, Professor *Tejan Waszak*
and husband *Kevin.*

Your encouragement helped
turn my dreams into reality.

Appreciation

Special thanks to the wonderful staff of
Tate Publishing & Enterprises.

It was a challenging task to arrange my
broken pieces into this exquisite masterpiece.
But they made it seemed effortless.

Your work is deeply appreciated.

Thank you all.

Table of Contents

Introduction.....................................15
The Strength I Did Not Know I Had 16
Smile..18
New Lease on Life...............................20
The Best Song of All.............................22
Stand with Me...................................24
Family Legacy 28
Just Shine 30
Grace..32
Gazing at Graffiti................................34
Happy Monday..................................36
Attitude Admired 38
The World of Works..............................42
I Am Like My Hair 44
Family Tree 48
How Would You Like to Be Remembered? 52
The Greenest Thumb 54

Encounter with Police	56
Dreams Never Die	60
What I Like about My House	62
Thank You, Lilly	64
The Face of "Me"	66
True Confession	70
Help the Needy	72
Oh! Mama	74
No! Listen Up	78
Caring Mom	82
Why Did He Hurt My Daughter?	84
Sing Me a Love Song	86
Second Chance	88
Island in the Sun	90
Role Model	94
I love NY	96
We Are His Bride	100
Face It or Face Up	102
Essence of Time	104
Earthen Garden	106
Don't Drink and Drive	110
What's Cooking?	112
Foreclosure: A Monster (Part One)	114
One Stop Store: the Cross	116

Inspiration	118
Long-Distance Loving	120
Glowing, Musical Tides	124
The World Is Your Stage	130
Love Your Heart	132
My Music	134
When the Day Rises	136
Portrait of an Artist	138
In My Heart	142
Foreclosure, You Monster (Part Two)	144
The Best Gift of All	148
Safer Zone	150
Happy Face	152
Like It Is	154
Imagine Tomorrow	156
The Passage of Time	158
My Special World	160
Longevity	162
Dare Not Compare	164
Difference Embrace	166
Hearts in the Past	168
Letter to My Daughter	174
Celebrate	176
Face to the Voice	178

Hello, Graduates	180
Graduates, Friends, and Family	182
Leave a Better Planet	188
See the Light	190
Overcoming Grief	192
Indelible Images	194
My Web and TV Savvy Parents	196
Flowers without Borders	198
One White Glove	202
Respect	206
Buckle up	208
Internet Spiders	210
Dear Mom and Dad	212
The Phoenix	216
Love Is	220
Musical Rose	222

Introduction

I am writing this book to share my experiences with readers.

I hope that they will become more focused on issues that affect our daily life.

They may be better able to face reality, in a more positive light.

As a mother and retired teacher from the beautiful Caribbean island of Jamaica,

I cherish the opportunity to provide guidance for young people. Going to school nowadays to receive an education is very important. It is quite difficult to care for one's family without earning a decent salary. Education is power. It will help you to get a job. It is better to have a certificate or diploma and no job, than no certificate or no diploma and no job.

I hope you will have as much fun reading this book as I did writing it.

THE STRENGTH I DID NOT KNOW I HAD

Did not know my strength.
Never thought I could win the fight.
I was faced with a negative situation.

Almost gave up on myself;
It took a good while
Until I came to realize.

Life is worth living.
Talked to myself, and in my dreams.
Looked in the mirror, it doesn't lie.

Thinking, concentrating, determine,
Affirming, reassuring,
Ignited my dream goals.

Got to keep moving, moving forward;
Resist sliding back.
Stand firm on solid ground.

It was a hard road I travelled;
A rough way to go.
I won't turn back,
No, I won't go back.

Talking to my inner-man,
Help me to understand
The strength I didn't know I had.

No matter what your downfall,
Don't let that be your last call.
Talk to your inner man.
The one who understands.

SMILE

You have that smile,
Innocent and kind.
Adorning the world,
So humble and divine.
A dawning new day.

Always a delight,
Just to see you smile.
Don't have to try,
It's all in your eyes,
A dawning new day.

You shared with the world,
The door to your soul.
When the time seemed dull and gloomy,
Smiles glow like starry nights.
A dawning new day.

What's your confession?
Heart songs you must share,
A dawning new day.

NEW LEASE ON LIFE

Believe it, claim it.
Affirm it, and regain.
Lord, give me
A new lease on life.

I need a new start.
It takes a big heart.
There is no shame in that.
I got a new lease on life.

Grab the bull by the horn,
Seek out higher learning.
Get the big backpack with my learning tools.
I got a new lease on life.

Jump on the bus, or train.
Go back to school.
Get some quality education,
That will land me in a job.
I got a new lease on life.

Pay attention to the teacher.
Learn a lot more in less time,
Cram it!
I got a new lease on life.

Whether you made a mistake,
End up in jail, or, like me,
At an early age, have a baby.
I got a new lease on life.

Some will find fault,
I won't halt.
Cares not what others say.
I got a new lease on life.

Praise and criticism go hand in hand.
Just be very glad,
I got a new lease on life.

THE BEST SONG OF ALL

Composition,
Dedicate to myself,
Impulsation.
What better way to start the day?

Not really about my feelings,
Just about time, places, and things.
Highlights of the beautiful day.
No special message, art and melody.

Humming while working,
Sing freely in the shower,
Feel empowered.
Composition from the soul.

Inspirational vibes,
Not only what's visible
Body moves with
Nature heart and soul.

Mixing my world.
Words flow like the river,
River of Babylon.
The best song of all.

But different from the band
Songs intensify, blend the tone.
News of the day, Local international.
Sing like a robin, wild and free.

Rap about nature, life is real.
Chant or recite, give myself advice.
Pick up where I left off.
Agreeing, neutral, and opposing

Heirloom of musical industry.
Imagination soars,
Positive notes evoked.
Then gone with the wind.

Not about fame, CDs, or big record deals;
No contract to read and seal.
Impulse of the soul composed,
Calms my world.

Sing your song, sing out loud.
Or sing it in your soul.
Simmer up a pleasant mood,
Soothe your way through the day.

STAND WITH ME

You are my hands, my feet, my eyes.
We will carve our laughter, hopes and visions,
Upon the face of solid rocks.
Your dreams, my schemes will
surely turn into reality
On the beach I will not stand
And write our plans upon the sand.

"Hard work and sacrifice,
Live within our means.
We must all invest in our future."
Solution that will serve all mankind.
Answers to everyday issues,
Faith and courage are within ourselves.

Let's go beyond, upon the wings of eagles bold.
We will kiss the cheeks of the Rushmore guys,
And carve our plans on solid rocks.
Look to the mountain top,
Where the King's dreams lie
See their dreams, our vision come to life.

A leap year comes every four,
We must seize this hour

And tackle our chores.
The wind will bear me on your wings,
A journey of excellence.

Like a precious gift unfold,
The best is yet to come.
"It takes a miracle to hold the world in space."
Let's look beyond the mountaintop.
Run every mile to the finish
Stand with me.

One final note,
"If your ideas are better than ours,
You are welcome."

How would we know if
Our ideas are better than yours?
Better than yours,
Ya, better than yours.

Weigh it,
Oh, Weigh it!

With what shall we weigh it?
Shall we weigh it?

Weigh it, with what?

Prayers of truth and honesty within oneself.

Lord,
Restore our souls in the valley;
That we may stand strong on the mountain,
In the valley, restore my soul.

FAMILY LEGACY

I am a part of the unending chain.
My family legacy.
It's not what you may think it is,
Money in the bank, house, or land.
It's the family names,
Passed on to me from ancestors,
Maternal and paternal.

When anyone in my family is successful,
Our whole family shared the happiness.
Success, failure, anything,
We are in this together.
It's family affair.

I promise to always protect and preserve,
The names, of which I am apart.
First, I will try to make better,
My personal life.
By striving to be the best
I can possibly be.
Stay focused,
Choose friends wisely,
Stay away from situations that
I don't want to be in.

Never be distracted from my lessons,
By video games, or anything else.

Be a good role model, work smart,
give back to my community.
No one can stop the crows from
Flying overhead;
Certainly, we can prevent them,
From nesting in our hair.
Names are a part of my family legacy.

JUST SHINE

Why worry of what I am lacked,
Covering my light,
When I can shine?
It's not my,
Mother, father, siblings, or friends.
It's about me.

Matters not
If I was born with a deformity.
Or something tragic happens,
And I ask "why?"
How awesome, I beat the odds,
Imagine, left millions of sperms and eggs behind.
Mother carried me for nine long months.

Spurred into this world, a bundle of joy.
I am here for a good reason.
To be able to,
Work with what I have,
Is a great opportunity.
There will be challenges.
I can shine, and I will.

"If I could, I would!" is a self-pity cry.
Nothing can hold me back, but myself.
The heart, mind, and soul.

Give it strength and faith,
I'll be empowered.

I can still sit in my wheelchair
And play ball.
Tell a child,
"Pay attention to,
What the teacher teaches,"

Or remind them,
"Stay away from trouble.
Lace sneaker, pull up, button up.
Have a great day!"

There in my wheelchair,
I can enjoy nature,
Watch the Bumble bees,
Float from flower to flower.
Pick a rose,
And have lots of young school friends.
There is great joy,
In the little things we do.

"The blind man in the dark,
Lighted his lamp;
The light is for others not to
Stumble over him."

GRACE

Grace. It is a girl's name,
Grace. It's a family name.
Another word for mother.
She took care of me,
With such grace and dignity.

Grace is an amazing word.
It's used in graceful ways.
"God of grace,
Goodness gracious,
Lord, give me grace."
I am grateful to see another day.

Grace is a gospel song
I love to sing.
"Amazing grace, how sweet the sound."
Grace is the thanks I give,
Before I have my meals.

Grace is a divine feeling.
It makes me feel more comfortable,
When I'm striving to do
The things I should.

GAZING AT GRAFFITI

Emotions overcome,
By the graphics in the art.
There is a mystic kind of feeling,
Embedded in my heart.
It imparts emotion that tells,
We'll never ever part.
Gazing at graffiti,
Messages impart.

I see hope, I see courage,
I see love and one who cared.
Your face I saw in every boy and girl.
Never had a chance to share,
The dreams they hold dear.

We shared the best years,
Sacred were those days.
Precious memories-
How they linger.
Inspired me to move on.

Remember when I said,
Can't see the forest,
Because of the big old trees.

You said, "Look, Ma!
It's a forestry of beautiful trees."
We had a blast. Ha, ha, ha!
Our laughter echoed in the forest.

You helped me to see life in a new light.
Man make Apollo, skyscrapers, computers
"Only God can make a tree"
You brought back sunshine in my life.

Gazing at community graffiti,
Sends a story to my soul.
The time we spend together is treasured art,
Instilled in my heart.
Abstract pictures stir memories never told.
Gazing at graffiti is a blessing in disguise.

HAPPY MONDAY

Getting out of bed,
Monday morning used to be difficult.
No! no more of those days.

It's Monday! Happy Monday.
Exciting school or work week.
Begin the day on a happy note,
Rap a rhythm, recite a poem,
The Twenty-Third Psalm,
Or something else.

I am so clean,
Fresh like the ocean breeze.
Perfumed soap-on-the-rope,
Or shampoo for soap.
No excuse.
The shower has the power,
To rejuvenate my body.

Oh! I am like a rose
In Martha's garden.
Dressed appropriate like my associates.
Mirror on the wall of my heart,

Tell me,
"Does my smile reflect my character?"

Oatmeal porridge, or cereal,
For breakfast;
Tapped on top in harmony,
Banana, strawberries.
Sparkling glass of orange juice,
Freshly squeezed from the box.
Catch up with the news while I chew.

Lunch in my go green Tupperware,
Nutritious, delicious and presentable.
Add a little extra, others might be near,
Little is much, when given from the heart.

Glance at my watch
It's past 8 o'clock.
Make sure I have all the necessities.
No one is available at the moment,
Leave a message.
Hooray! Happy Monday.

ATTITUDE ADMIRED

A great attitude is invaluable.
I am happy,
I have the freedom to do great things.
To cultivate a good attitude is a gift.
It is very important in our daily lives.
First, love and proper care for myself.
Respect for people and property.

When I portray the right attitude,
It gives a sense of comfort in whatever I do.

Responsibility, accountability, and humility;
Are all attributes to attitude.
I try to incorporate these values,

In my daily life.
It helps me to be more successful in,
Education, work, and play.
Great in social life.

I treat others,
As I would like them to treat me.
"Please, excuse, I am sorry,
Please forgive me."
Teacher says,
"It takes a real person to say those words."
Each of us has the choice to
Have a positive attitude.

The uniqueness of attitude is:
We take it wherever we go.
It is easily pronounced.
Others can adopt our attitude.
There is always room for improvement.

Life is said to be ten percent action,
And ninety percent reaction.
My associates may not remember
The expensive shoes,
The beautiful clothes I used to wear.
They will remember my reaction,
When I was treated unfairly.

Even if I did not say a word;
My body language sends a strong message.

We may not be able to control the inevitable,
But we can embrace,
Graceful attitude toward every situation.
"Attitude Admired."

THE WORLD OF WORKS

In this world
We need a skill
Or a good education.
Beat failure with success.
Be prepared and take the test.

Climb the ladder of success;
Take whatever you can get.
Move on until you find fulfilment.
Better to have an education and,
Can't get a job;
Than no certificate or diploma and,
Oh, no job.
If at first you don't succeed,
Try, try, and try again.

A great sports master once said,
"I was tired of failing,
That is how I succeeded."
The sky is the limit.
We can do it.

Better to be the man at the door
Than the one on the corner.

The one on the corner does
A very bad thing.
He tried to sell some illegal drugs,
The police got him.
But the man at the door
Gives you correct information.
Even helps you with your bags.
Coming in from the heat or cold.

In every work environment,
We need to know a few things.
Utilize every opportunity for
Higher education.
Check out the free stuff;
In-service is a must.
Be prepared, next in line,
Promotion may be in the air.
Don't get angry if it's not your season.

Give credit to your, company.
It's where your pay-checks coming from.
Maintain a good work relationship.
They are our nine-to-five work family.
We will work in harmony.

I AM LIKE MY HAIR

Girls like me spend quality time
Trying different styles.
We choose to keep those we like
Only if they look right.
Photographic memories of various styles
Embedded in our minds.
I am like my hair.

As a result of illness or hereditary,
I sometimes lose my hair.
I can wear a wig or go bare.
The choice is up to me.
See, it's not what's on my head that matters.

It's the head that makes my decisions.
I am like my hair.

I wear each style on different occasions,
Appropriate for the call.
Some styles I wear up and some down,
Short, tall, straight, or curly,
They all seemed to fit just right.
I like my hair.

Sometimes I style it myself at home;
Other times I go to the salon.
Textures soft, kinky, smooth, or silky.
Hair can be a work of art.
I am like my hair.

I would not consider it "a bad hair day"
When a style I like just doesn't seem right.
Or I may be out of time to press or curl
After I have washed.
In fact, it's an opportunity I embrace,
To show off what's on top.
I am like my hair.

Colourful, bandana, caps, and hats,
Caps with logos that read:
"Proud to serve a veteran,"
"Someone in Florida loves me,"
"I love New York,"

Not one that says, "Bad hair day."
I am like my hair.

Head - ties, caps, and hats are the cutting edge,
Precious commodities.
They are ahead of our time,
Will remain hat long after we are gone.
I am like my hair.

Me, my hair, have in common,
Growing strength and beauty.
The greatest differences are:
I am growing daily in love,
Wisdom, knowledge, and understanding.
My hair changes style every day.
I like my hair.

The values I hold dear
Will remain the same.
No matter what I am going through
They will never change.
I am like my hair,

But I'm much more than just my hair.

FAMILY TREE

My family and trees are so much alike;
Every time I see a magnificent tree,
It reminds me of my family.
Strong, grounded, and beautiful.
Each part of a tree represents us.

Grandparents are the roots.
Well grounded.
They stand firm in their beliefs.
And make sure we do the same.
"Make sure your hands are clean before you eat."
Grandma says.

"Stay out of trouble now."
Grandpa's favourite advice.

I am sentimentally attached to the
Trees, close to my home:
Palms, Oak, Redwood and Maples.
Their sturdy trunks
Are my view of parents' assurance,
Their love and guidance.

Those special trees,
Like Mom and Dad;
They have been there,
Years before I was born.
Sometimes I throw my weak arms,
Around a big, tall trunk.
Say a prayer,
Then I feel strong.
I feel free to hug my parents any time.
Even after they scolded me for doing wrong.

Sprawling branches with crossing limbs,
We never always see eye to eye.
Family ties
Swaying leaves dancing in the air.
Sometimes,
They touched.

Aunts, uncles, cousins, brothers and sisters.
We hug.

Like an array of trees in the forest
There is unity in diversity.

It's not just me,
My parents too, are fond of trees.
Guess what? My name, like a tree,
Mahogany.
Parents vision of
Strength, beauty and reselliance.
How awesome can trees be.

Trees, like my family, spell "Love."

HOW WOULD YOU LIKE TO BE REMEMBERED?

I would like to be remembered by:
Warm hugs and kisses kind and true.
Especially those that I embraced,
When my days seemed blue.
My admiration for beauty in,
People, places, and things.
Birds, animals, and flowers.
Even the silver raindrops,
And the red sparks in the blazing fire.

I would like to be remembered by:
Decisions that I made that,
Turned out to be fair or wise.
The things that I treasured
In my childhood years.
Such as going to church and school.
Things that my parents taught me to do.
They certainly guided me through my life.

I would like to be remembered by:
Not the home that I own, cars I drive,
And clothes that I wear;
But for those whom I really care.

Orphans, the homeless, the sick and needy.
Victims of forgotten justice.

I would like to be remembered by:
What I learned from—
Parents, teachers, preachers,
Dreamers, leaders, and followers.

Most of all,
I would like to be remembered by:
What I am learning from you.

THE GREENEST THUMB

My vegetable garden is a knock out!
"You have the greenest thumb I ever saw,"
My neighbours said.
"How does your garden grow?"
No Silver Bells or Cockle shells,
Nor pretty girls all in a row.
I am gifted to do great gardening.
I have the greenest thumb

I spend happy hours,
Weeding, planting, amending and watering.
They thrive,
Hefty banana plants embracing the sky.
Plush green spinach, creeping high.
I have the greenest thumb

My garden is a rainbow of colours–
Living colours.
Green foliage of tender string beans
Gold, green, and bold stripe pumpkins–
Pretty, just like Cockle shells.

Big Bell peppers, red, green and yellow.
Swinging faster than silver bells.

Huge royal purple egg-plant,
One of a kind.
Reminds me of the movie
"Colour Purple."

Sweet red ripe tomatoes,
Like pretty girls, all in a row.

Exotic aromas,
Steamed from beaming blossoms,
Blast through open windows,
Like tsunami throughout my house
Tantalising fragrance leave behind.

Welcome guests,
The birds and the bees,
Squirrels and insects.
Feast upon my delicious crops.
After my friends and neighbours
Have had their lots

I like to watch while they eat and flop.
When on my window sill they propped.
Leaving their droppings behind.
"Tweet, tweet," they tweeted me.
"That's good manure."

ENCOUNTER WITH POLICE

Police that I know
Help to bring positive change.
They are firm enough to do the job,
Compassionate to treat us right.
They patrol and protect,
Not stop and harass.
If it wasn't for the law, men would
Govern themselves and try to rule others.

Next time you are driving,
Have run-in with the law,
Don't pull out your cell
Call no anyone.
They'll think it's a gun
You are reaching for.
Stay still in your vehicle,
Don't even breathe
Until they get to you.

If you know you're in the right.
Where are you running to?
Who are you going to?
Stand up, hands up, face up.

It's your right, to know your rights.

Watch your back while running
To catch the bus or train.
Especially if you live in
Certain parts of the city.
They might think you
Committed a crime,
Running from the scene.

Zooming through stop light,
Can't have that!
You could wipe out
The breadwinner in the family.
Leave little children without parents.

If you are caught speeding
On a slow lane,
Show remorse, be respectful.
They may sympathize.
"To err is human; to forgive is divine."

Threatening, resisting, running
Doesn't make it right.
Just do what they say.
They are of the law.
"To obey is better than sacrifice."

Keep a clean slate.
Ignorance of the law,
Is no excuse.

DREAMS NEVER DIE

Pictures hung high adorned the wall,
Strong faces of global endurance.
Men and women standing tall.
Mandella, Rosa Parks,
Dr. Martin Luther King Jr.
Marcus Garvey.

We are living the dreams
For which they fought.
Liberty, Freedom, Life.

Astronauts,
The military, fire fighters,
Policemen and women,
Medical workers, teachers.
All positive contributors to society.
Everyday heroes,
The center of our universe.
Behind some faces are the grim reality of
Death and war.

Your pictures may not be
Embellished by frames on any wall,

With much pride and honour,
You are treasured in our hearts.
All together brave.

Memories of strength and courage,
"Blissful contentment measured."
Dreams never die, but usher us on.
Do good "by any means necessary."
Your picture may be engraved
On someone's heart;
A badge of honour.

WHAT I LIKE ABOUT MY HOUSE

Within the walls is love and unity.
The peace that reins within
Is an invaluable gift.

I dearly admire, vaulted ceiling,
Beautiful furniture and appliances.
What I like best are the folks
Who live here.

I would not care less
If my bed was the floor,
I was never served
My favourite dish of fish and chips,
Or delicious pumpkin pie.
As long as everyone is happy, that's all I care.

What if someone spills something?
We clean that up without a fuss.
My children all around me.
Some of them with runny nose.
Little Junior without pants and shirt,
Dipping in my dish while we hug and kiss.

Baby Jasmine,
Like the flowers in our garden,
Just as sweet as she can be.

I'm not annoyed if she cries.
I hush her, and sing sweet lullaby,
"Have you ever seen a Lap-wing bird?"

We lie around on the floor,
Tell stories,
The children catch up on their lessons.
I comb their hair,
We fold the clothes
Then we strip corn and shell peas.

My soul mate in the kitchen
Frying chicken, not forgotten.
Occasionally, I pop in.
Surprise smooches, tap on the shoulder.
The children like to see us display affection
Toward each other.

The coolest thing about marriage,
I live in blissful harmony
With my best friend.
"Home sweet home."
"Seldom is heard a discouraging word."

The love that we share
Surpassed issues disagreed.
I am not much, but they are all mine.
Home, where the last kiss never ends.

THANK YOU, LILLY

The Lilly Act for equal labour, equal pay.
I am not mad,   as a matter of fact,
I am glad.
Men and women, equal labour, equal pay.

Lilly, you stood up for the rights,
The rights for
Mothers, sisters, and daughters.
No one should fuss or fight if
If his wife's pay check is equally right.
At last! men and women;
Equal labour, equal pay.

Since we do not have to work so much overtime
To make ends meet.
We can now afford to spend quality time
As a family.
Take a vacation once in a while.
That is what I'm telling you, man.
Live life to the fullest.
Is one life I have.
Budget our time and money wisely,
And it will make sense.

Lilly, your name will go down in history, my dear.
Not as the Lilly of the valley, but
The Lilly Act that supports
Equal labour, equal pay for men and women.

Come on honey,
Now, let's go to bed—an, an, and,
Celebrate the Lilly act,
How to spend our additional money.
Thank you President Obama,
For signing the act into law.
More money for my honey.

THE FACE OF "ME"

Dear Cupid,
As you noticed, I was not at school today,
We both missed out in so many ways.
I imagine
You looked high; you looked low.
Others pretended it was a puppet show.
Disappointment raised its ugly claws
When you could not find me

Without a question, they all knew.
The poison arrow missed its bow.
They sighed, they reckoned,
Some shed silent tears.
Aw! My head hurts

I wanted to be there so badly,
But the fear was more than I could bear.

This little head of mine
Played like a bouncing ball
Against the cold hard wall.
Often times I wished that
Your big, strong arms would be tired soon

Even though I did not go to school today,
I felt as if I was there.
You tumbled after me in hot pursuit.
A starving hawk upon its prey.

Threw me high, you threw me low.
Round and round you swing me.
How much can a rag doll bear?
Aw! My head hurts.
How quick your happy kicking feet compete.
Like the shiny pedals on my bicycle
When I am racing to the finish line.

I curled up like a fetus,
With my hands covered my face.
In my mother's womb.
Oh! How I wish that I was still there.
I would never, ever leave.

However, I must be at school tomorrow.
If I stayed home; I'd be just like you,
Allowing some feeble child
To endure the horror that was meant for me.
Instead of them, I will be there for you;
A timid mouse yield to a hawk.

I ensured their happiness.

Your bitter cup they will not take.
When they see my humble face.
They all know that, I am your beating post.
Aw! my whole body aches.

The names that you teased me are not bad at all.
I read them in the Bible—frog, cry, baby, fat, pig.

The things that puzzled me most are:
The messages from your eyes.
The way you flipped your nose,
when you look at me.
What's up with the middle finger?
Can it not bend like the rest?
Let's all try to get along.
Love,
Me

TRUE CONFESSION

Check this out!
I'd rather be organized
Than disorganized and stressed.
My home is not the neatest, but
I know where the important things are.
Most things are where they ought to be.
A place for everything and
Everything in its place.

If things are not where they're supposed to be,
Precious time is wasted looking, looking.
When a place is cluttered.
You find other things that you
were not looking for.
Then totally forgot what is it
you are trying to find.

When I see on TV clutter at someone's house,
Then I'm glad it's not my house.
At the end of the day,
Most of the things are put away.
Guess who used to do it? Had to be Mom.

"I prefer to do it myself," she says,
"Than repeatedly ask."
The last time she said that
I jumped in and helped.
Now the rule is, "If you spill it, clean it."
Guess who doing it now? Everyone helps.

HELP THE NEEDY

Rich or poor,
It's good to give to those in need.
"It's better to give than to receive.
There is a special blessing
For those who share.

Earthquake, tsunami,
Other natural disasters,
It is not just an historical event
That will go behind.
It is a call for us to care.

"God has no hands but ours,
On us he can rely."

OH! MAMA

How strong your influence is on me.
Although I'm grown,
Your advice still sounds.
Now I understand.
Like it was,
Still is.

Your sweet voice,
Like perfume in the air,
Lingers in my ears,
Telling me,
"When you go out,
Have to make a good impression.
First one is the best.

It will even last the longest.
Might never get a chance to make another."
Ma! How true and strong are your words.
It certainly works for me.

Oh! Mama,
Wonderful words still echoing in my ears.
Sometimes I just add a musical tone.
"Always comb your hair,
Wear clean underwear,
Brush teeth is a must.
Run and catch the bus.

Take your learning tools,
When you go to school.
Treat others good and it will come back to you.
"Excuse, please, and thank you," always work.
Make peace instead of fuss and fight.
Be true to yourself.

Oh! Mama,
Your voice perfumed the air,
Just like when I was a kid.
You never like to see me cry,
Wipe the tears from my eyes.
Never miss PTA,

Teacher said I was a C.
You encouraged me to shoot for A.
Despite labelled alphabet,
Did my very best,
Never failed a test.

Now I'm grown, on my own.
Dressed appropriate.
Take my tools to work.
Always do my very best.
Like a baby, cradled on it's mother's breast,
I will forever live in your warm embrace.

There is something about my taste buds that
Relates back to your kitchen.
Oh! Delicious home-cooking.
You know much I love your apple pies.
Sometimes that nostalgic mood
Just wrapped me like a blanket,
Covered me in field of dreams.
Breakfast, lunch and supper time,
Then I'm lifted to your kitchen in sweet aroma.

Oh memories, how vivid,
Written in my heart book of the chronicles,
All through the years.
Thank you for everything you've done.

The beautiful bouquet on this letter
I sprayed with my lavender perfume.
I would like you to enjoy the
Lovely fragrance
While you still can.
I love you, Mom.

NO! LISTEN UP

No is no, because it's so.
No is no, night or day.
Sun or rain, no is no.
"No! Don't touch that."
You stepped back.
Learned that as a baby.

Now you are grown,
When someone tells you "No,"
The same thing you do;
Like a baby, step back.

My body language says No,
And my voice says No.
What in "NO" don't you understand?

"No," when I am crying is No.
"No," when I am beaming is No.
Laughing No or hell No!

If I say yes at first and no after,
It means "No."
I have the right to change my mind.

Listen up!
No matter who you are,
Or where you go,
"No," is always "NO."
"No" is a universal language,
Everyone should understand.

Teacher Walker, Student Palker.
Mr. and Mrs, Harper.
Mothers and fathers, sons and daughters.
Lawers, docters, Indians chiefs.
Men, women, boys and girls.
Rich or poor.
Black or white,
Friend or foe,
Pimp, pope and pauper,
John Hancock or some little brat.

If someone tells you, "No," don't react.
Be civilized, respect that.
Just like when you were a baby.
You understood, and stepped back.

Next time you are having problem with the "N0."
Acting like you don't know.
Check out the hands.
You'll understand.

Double reminder in the palms of your hands.
"NO" naturally tattooed for you.
It may look like letters "M, Y, or F" failing grade.
Call it what you may.
Look again.
This is what it is.
Visible "N," and invisible "O."
It spells "No,"

Listen up.
If you are having problem with the "No."
Talk to the hands.
Or be like a baby.
Step back.
This time, in someone else's shoes.

CARING MOM

Stay out of trouble, listen to a double,
Like a mom.
No look-a-like, just the good "Old book,"
There for you any time, my child, day or night.
Never wink, never sleep, read as you please.
Legitimate advice that may save lives.
Rich supply of
Love, thoughts, and rules of conduct.

Need not stress over a cheating lover.
Cheating lovers are everywhere.
Unfaithful lovers are not just yesterday.
They are like paper roses;
How real they seemed to be.

Be careful of whom you tell your business
There is hate, jealousy, and grudge.
Never listen to gossip.
The same one who brings you news
Will take it back,
And not the way it was said.
The aim may be for you to lose your cool,
Act like a fool, break off with boo,
So they could take your place.

Never be overcome by jealousy.

It's a green-eyed monster,
No time to think.
A crooked voice that triggers you
To do wrong.
Anger makes you feel heated at the moment,
And bitter later.

Never make anyone the subject of
Your physical or verbal abuse.
"Hot tempered is infectious,
Don't get infected."
Beware of emotional moments.
"Here's my hands,
This my pout,
When I'm steamed up I will shout."

Follow your heart.
Learn to recognize the difference in the voice,
Think before you act.
It doesn't matter if you have to
Lock yourself in your room and cry.
With your cell phone, maybe,
Be glad you're not in a cell bed.
Stay safe.

WorldWide Caring Mom.
Proverb 3: 5–6.

WHY DID HE HURT MY DAUGHTER?

She is under eighteen
With the dream of learning a life skill
Or going to college.
A feeling of independence.
She has a bright future, lots of opportunity;
Loans, grants,
Father who loves her.
Why would anyone want to mess that up.

Smartha is the smartest girl I know,
A student.
Happy, happy little girl,
Loving and affectionate.
What do you mean, you are pregnant?
That can't be,
Strip shows blue,
Doctor confirmed it's true.
Tell me you are joking blues.

I made sure I drove you to school,
Pick you up, take you home.
You sat patiently in my office
Until I finished overtime.
We were always together.

People always tell us that.
I gave you everything.

He hurt my daughter.
She is too young,
Having a baby.
Can't help these tears from
Fall, fall-falling
Tough guy like me,
Shouldn't be cry, cry-crying.
I am a cop,
Those little punk should be afraid of me.

We should have moved into a jungle,
Live in a tree house.
Or maybe to a convent,
There we could only hear the clanging of bells,
The chanting of nuns, like Mother Therisa.

Why! Why me?
I fought long and hard
Won custody from a loving mother,
Just for Smartha to have a better life.
This little girl,
Nothing, Nothing,
I want nothing to happen to my little girl.
The same thing happened to her mother.
But the clock turned back at me
Fifteen years ago.

SING ME A LOVE SONG

Sing me a song,
A love song.
We know the words we like to hear.
How much it cheers
Sweetens the atmosphere.

Heart to heart,
"You are my one and only.
Sweet Caroline."
Never mind the melody
Words of love come naturally.

"Happy today'
Happy together,
Happy forever."
Ignite our love through emotion,

Hug, like we'll never let go,
Dance, as if there's no tomorrow
Feel, the warmth of our embrace.
Taste, the honey romance.
Kisses on and on,
"Life is a song, sing on."

SECOND CHANCE

Give me a second chance, not
only in love but in life.
I made a mistake when I was young. Yes, I did,
Nothing to be proud of.
I committed a crime,
And I served the time.

Reintegrate me; help to educate me.
The institution already shaped me,
Put me back into society.
I can build bridges, railroads, and highways,
Drive trucks and buses,
Maintain parks, good at art, and I am very smart.

Not a dollar in my pocket,
One suit on my back,
No roof overhead.
Only a record to my name,
Not the one that you play,
Over 'n over and again-n-again,
It's the one that caused you to be ashamed.
Like a shadow, it follows you for life.

Please help me with a job.
I don't want to go back to that,
Society, please take me back.
I would like to give back and interact,
Only one more chance.
I will prove to you I'm a good man.
Hope you will understand.
Like the potter and the clay,
The Master is leading me a new way.

I asked not to be judged on a single incident.
But on the manifest intention of my entire life.

ISLAND IN THE SUN

Save up enough dough,
Vacation time in the air!
Take your cell and suitcase.

Get some cool clothes—shorts,
T-shirts and jeans,
A card and little cash.
Fly bravely on the iron bird.
Get there fast and hang-out slow.

Dress up when you want to party;
Dress down to feel the ocean breeze.
Forget about work, school, and paying bills.
Deal with that when you come back.

All countries are nice, real, real nice.
Sometimes we need to slide, get-away.
Experience another.
How about that?
"Come to Jamaica and feel all right."
If you are grown boy or girl,
Here in Sunny-Isle,
We all are One.

Enjoy the ocean front,
Lay back have fun.
No cold, no snow, no worries at all,
The tropical breeze, in awe! you feel.
Blue-green turquoise water,
White sandy beaches.

Special dish, Ackee and salt fish,
Lobster, crayfish, fish and ockro,
Boiled green banana, yellow yam, cornival.
Delicious carrot juice, strong-back,
Coconut water, Sea moss and linseed.
Red Stripe beer, is not red
And has no stripes.
Please yourself, chefs appease.

Of course not ! You don't have to drive.
You are A tourist!
Leave the driving to Slim and Fatty.
Pick up a slang or two–
"Yes man, no problem man, Irie."

Sensational rejuvenation,
Climb to heavenly heights
Dunns River Falls.
No problem man,
It's natural accommodation,

Swing slide, horseback ride.
Super attraction,
Dance the Rhumba,
Dirty Dandy and Miss Pansy.
Reggae, Hip hop and Dance hall.

Nuff-nuff hospitality, respect and love.
Jamaica is where you'd like to be.
Sweet memories until you go again.

ROLE MODEL

I am a role model—not a
Super model or a super star.
Nor do I drive a nice car.
I am a leader, not a follower.
Honesty, loyalty, sincerity, truth, and justice,
Those are some of the virtues I believe in.

My life is an example.
It is like a cupid bow,
Sends messages straight to the heart.
I Treat older women like a mother,
Younger ones as my sisters.
Every man and boy a brother.

"No man is an island;
No one stands alone."

Not a bit of boasting in my bones,
Just sharing what parents have taught me.
I am a good worker,
Also a great student.
I do not need anyone to watch over me
For the dollars that I earn or the grades I deserve.
I work to the best of my ability.

Assisting others when I can,
Ask questions of what I do not understand.
Willing to lend a hand,
Associates are reminded,
I am here if you need me.
I am only a phone call away.

I LOVE NY

New York, New York.
The city so nice they named it twice.
Skyscrapers kissing sky.
Night lights dazzle eyes.
I love New York.

No more twin towers,
But still the Empire.
Spectacular tree lighting,
The night before Christmas.
I love New York.

Broadway ahead,
Performing arts, shows and concerts.
"New York, Empire State of Mind."
Melodious song boasting the city.
New York is where
Many young adults would like to live,
Due to the high cost of living,
They seek out near boroughs,
Queens, Brooklyn, Statin Island and the Bronx.
I love New York.

The biggest melting pot,
Over flowing.
Like a crock pot, it keeps on bubbling.

Never refused anyone; homeless or billionaire,
Sure! You will find them there.
Faces from everywhere.
Migrating birds flying high,
Just like people all around.
Up town, downtown,
All God's land.
Business, study, work, or fun.
Age, race, creed, sexual orientation.
"Out of many we are one."
I love New York.

Folks on the go, fast not slow.
Yellow taxi cab, bound
East, west, north, and south.
Cash cab checking passengers IQs,
If you pass, Ya! Free ride and money.
Hap on, off triple double decker.
Jump on the subway, one low fare, ride all day.
Transportation 24x7.
Swing low like crows in cable cars.
Pay as you go on China man's bicycle.
Ferry to Statin Island and back,
Climb Lady Liberty, absorb history.
Cruse up and down the Hudson,
See more wonders of nature.

Clubs and institutions always in session,
New York University to Montissori.
Night or day is always light.
The city so bright, they named it twice.

Celebrity shopping,
Men in black.
Men who
Made off with someone's pocket book.
Turn a blind eye to any game that looks too good.
Not everyone is nice and friendly.
Men in blue, New York's finest,
There to help protect you.
New York, New York.

Have your own way,
From the Subway
To Broadway and the Runway.
Not everyone is met with success.
Beware of unfaithful lovers
Waiting to prance upon lonely faces.
New York, New York.

Lonely hearts fallow
Wolves in sheep's clothing.
First you start off dining, kissing,
Then maybe missing.
Adding to the statistics

Was not intended for you.
Leaving loved ones in turmoil.
For each light that burns in the city
There are families with broken hearts.
New York, New York.

Enjoy concerts in the subways:
Magicians, musicians, amateur artists.
I love New York.

Walk "Avenues of The Americas"
Horse and buggy tour.
Enjoy concerts in the subways:
Magicians, musicians, amateur artist,
Sight scene cable cars, hovering over the city
Swing low like crows.
Pay as you ride on China man's bicycle.
I love New York.

The rest is left for you to see.
New York, New York,
The city so nice they named it twice.
I love New York.

WE ARE HIS BRIDE

Our hearts are his thrones.
His promises clear,
Love, rich and pure.
We are his bride,
He is preparing a place for us,
Where he is,
We'll be there too some day.

His name is highly treasured,
The only name in which we find
Strength and salvation.

Be encouraged,
Rest on his words.
His eyes are on the little sparrows,
Much more on us.
He never leaves us or forsakes us.
"Footprints on the sand,"
Experiencing a bad or sad situation,
He carry us through.

Sing, Sing in our hearts,
"The Lord Is My Shepherd."
Hide them in our hearts,

"Wonderful words, beautiful words of life."
Like a well, draw from it,
In times of heartaches and pain,
It will quench the thirsting of our Soul.

FACE IT OR FACE UP

Our face takes us wherever we go.
It reflects our emotions:
Glad, sad, mad, pity, joy, pain.
It is vital that our face looks good.
Let's face it,
No matter what level of emotions
we are experiencing,
Outer beauty rates as high as good character.

The epitome of beauty
Cannot be defined by one specific answer.
Beautiful in one country but
Plain in another.
The definition alters
Depending on culture and style.

It doesn't matter who we are,
It is important to be noticed
Even as we get older.
Duty in beauty,
Keep things simple, clean, and fresh.

Face best assets,
Eyes are windows to the soul.

An expression of smile
Transcend time and place.
Your beautiful face.

Face up,
Achieving maturity without showing
Visible signs of facial aging,
Is a strongly held aspiration.

Face it,
We see the face,
God sees the heart.

ESSENCE OF TIME

Time.
Precious little four letter word,
Yet biggest impact on our lives.
Everlasting.
Reason for the seasons.
Universally used and embraced.

Time is abstract,
Accepted, respected,
For you to waste or embrace.
Never stand still, going, no turning back.
Time is coming up soon,
For something you have to do.
"What time is it?" someone asked.
Can't store it, adore it, enjoy it in happy times.

Babies demand it,
Children take it,
Mothers love it.
Sometimes we excuse it,
Use it, and abuse it.
"Watch or clock" It is about time.
Numbers one through twelve are magical,

Limited yet infinite,
Morning, noon, evening, and night.
Time is like money; use it wisely.

EARTHEN GARDEN

Weeding, planting, tending,
Earthen garden for success.
Sowing through harvesting,
Earthen Garden inspires awe!
Spectacular blooming blossoms;
Colours: lavender, pink, red, white and blue.
Delicious edibles, year after year.

Tempting fruits, swaying in the air,
Stayed fresh in the cool breeze.
Mother earth keeps refrigerated:
Carrots, beets, turnips, potatoes,
Till straight from the garden to the kitchen.

Earthen Garden arose the senses,
Unique activities of garden friends:
Squirrels go nuts,
Flirting grasshoppers, friendly ladybugs,
Dancing butterflies.
Gaze at the changing colours,
Blue-grey sky, purple-green hills,
Meandering red river through the rocks.

There is no other feel like
The cool mountain breeze,
Mother earth wafted sweet fragrance all over me
Stones wrapped in soil mingled with
Sage, parsley, leaves from everywhere.
I began to think, the best perfume is free.

Sit for a while on the rock,
Warm sunshine on my back.
Don't need clock or watch
To show me time,
I can tell from the position of the sun or
My shadow.

Dew drops trickling from a leaf,
Soft melody,
Busy bumble bees familiar zees,
Cock-a-doodle-doo, dominator rooster.

Hummingbirds dancing, wings rotating,
Robins tweeting,
Woodpecker rapping.

Delicious taste:
Red cherry tomatoes,
Strawberries and figs,
Fresh green lettuce,
Sweet strawberries.
Pick and eat, appetite appease.

Enjoy nature,
Natural exercise,
Share the prise.
Enhance a sense of pride.
Earthen garden rejuvenates
A state of mind.

DON'T DRINK AND DRIVE

There are many bars
That are not far
From the house where I was living.
I used to spend a lot of time
Drinking whiskey and chasing men.

I did not know my limit
Until all my drinks were finished.
Jumped into the driver's seat,
The road to Derick's house.

The car was speeding,
I was sleepy.
I was feeling kind-a dizzy.
The sky was upside down,
And my eyes were popping out.

I could not remember the difference
Between yield and merge.
Didn't even know, my car was out of control,

All I knew was
They were somebody's loved ones.

I could not see eye to eye
When I was DWI.

Take my advice,
Don't you ever drink and drive.
I will live with guilt for the rest of my life.

The victim's mother mourned,
"You make me 'MADD.'"

WHAT'S COOKING?

Elton, Brandon, and Nathon,
They will be home from school soon.
I would like to add something
Nutritious to their meals.

Mummy, Mummy we are home,
What's cooking?
Wait, wait! Don't tell me,
Where is the cookie jar?
Who moved the jar from the snack spot?

Boys, boys, calm down,
Change your clothes,
Wash your hands.
Pick a fruit from the basket until dinner is served,
Or have a glass of water.

No more see food, or fast food diet.
Today we'll start meals nutritious,
Brown rice and grilled chicken,
Wheat bread and Tofu is optional,
Delicious gravy on top.
Garden fresh
Brussels sprouts and tomatoes.

Who don't want that can have,
Wheat dumplings and green bananas,
Yam and potatoes,
Stew fish with okra.

Nature juice!
Blended beets, mangoes, cucumbers.
Just any fruit can be used.
Spice it up with ginger and nutmeg.

We can always mix the produce,
As long as we have
Less fats and sweets,
More vegetables and whole grain.
No changes, just
Less of the first and more of the second.
Special night out
Taco or pizza!

We love this new stuff.
Mom,
Speak the truth,
Who have you been hanging out with
Martha, Oprah, or the First Lady?

FORECLOSURE: A MONSTER (PART ONE)

Foreclosure is like a monster.
Not Cookie Monster, but
A real, huge, ugly monster.
It can get almost anyone, even me.

I worked very hard,
Living at Mama's house.
She said that I am grown,
Should be on my own.
I made sacrifices, saved my dollars.

Had my eyes on a nice big house,
Passed it every morning, on my way to work.
"For Sale" sign,
I knew then it was mine.

"Home Sweet Home,"
I sang all the way home.
Paid all my money down, and even got a loan.

Married my man, moved right in.
Soon we had twins.
My SUV. Plasma TV,

Everything spanking new,
With a nice panoramic view.

Soon after, lost my job couldn't find another,
Unemployment it seems took forever.
Then came the bills, piling up;
Car-notes, phone, cable, electric bills
Started to think, *What's up with that?*
Mortgage rate that escalates.
Never was a steady rate.

I said, Lova, let's make a financial plan.
But he didn't seem to understand,
"I owed child support and tickets to the court,"
Was his response.

Seems like we no longer can enjoy the view.
Foreclosure, you monster!
I am not giving up.
A girl will do what
A girl got to do.

ONE STOP STORE: THE CROSS

A one stop superstore.
There we can get anything
With credit card or cash.
Get our car tires changed
While we get our nails done,
Test prescription glasses,
Shop for food and clothes.

The cross on Calvary is like a one-stop shop.
Money is no good there;
Salvation is free.
He paid for our sins with his precious blood;
We must believe and have faith.

The cross has an indelible reflection on our hearts.
It's there in our hearts,
Our fears turn to hope.
He erased our depression,
Comforts our lonely, broken hearts.
He wiped our tears away.

Sometimes it's on our knees
Sins are forgiven,
Hearts made whole,

Souls restored.
The world cannot hold us down.
"Let my people go."
Say no to what's holding us back.
We'll will find peace with ourselves and others.
The cross can give us perfect peace.

INSPIRATION

I have enough inspiration
For self-motivation.
Some children have Mom and Dad
To encourage, motivate, and cheer them on.
Fact to face,
I am on my own, but I'm not alone.

Activate my intuitive.
I have potential.
Plus, I'm young, strong, and healthy.
I can succeed in whatever I focus on.

Bright future ahead, lots of opportunity.
A lesson from the old school.
Only a few were
"Born with a silver spoon to their mouth."
I am happy to be able to work
And provide for myself.

I am on my own, but not alone.
A higher hand is holding mine
Into the future.
Lighting the path and guiding my steps.

LONG-DISTANCE LOVING

When the lights are down in the city,
The stars shine brighter in the dark night,
I can feel your love all over me,
Although you are many miles away.
I am consumed by our love affair.
From my window,
The water in the bay seems like starlight
Because that's what you are to me.

I did not know what love is
Until I met you.
It's like falling in love
For the first and last time.
Some folks don't believe in long-distance loving.
Not even in holy matrimony.
A strong bond keeps us together.
Just like the old-fashion way.

Start on a clean slate,
Issues buried,
Before we get married.
I won't forget to tell you
There are children in my life.

True love grows,
Lovers apart,

Work, or,
Fighting war for peace.
I know some day we will be together,
Right here in my arms once again.
You will be with me in all my dreams.
Missing you, see you soon.

Darling, how much I anticipate your coming.
It's kind of a dating game we play.
Can't wait to get home from work
To talk on the phone once again.
Missing you, see you soon.

Flip and look at your pictures,
Sliding across the screen,
Like a game we play.
Honey, you swept me off my feet.
Wish the last kiss lasted longer.
Missing you, see you soon.

Just can't seem to say goodbye.
Thinking of you and about tomorrow.
Your caring attitude I savour,
On our coffee table is a flavour-
The Jasmine flower,
Like the fragrance of our romance,
Lingers long after you are gone.

Just can't seem to say good bye.

Tell me why you control me.
Its' not your charming face,
Your sexy body.
Have me thinking,
Your caring spirit,
And heavenly soul.
Miss you, see you soon.

Just can't seem to say goodbye,
How sweet your love is to me.
I like long-distance loving,
Until you get home to me.
There will be ups and down,
We are not perfect.
I promised it will be alright.
Recognizing our weakness and our strength
And how much we complement,
Miss you, see you soon.

I believe in long-distance loving.
You mean the world to me.
I heard you knocking at my door.
In my dreams,
Lonely, rainy nights.
Missing you, see you soon.

GLOWING, MUSICAL TIDES

Push! Pull!
Friendly tug of war,
Honeymoon or Senior prom.

Moon and ocean entertaining
Just like people celebrating.
Full moon the bride,
Greetings from the isle;
Ocean groomed,
In a heavenly mood;
Characters of loyalty.
Without both, there couldn't be a show.

Mrs. Full Moon and Mr. Oceanic Sphere
In their shining glory,
Like happy newly weds,
Yet way beyond compare.

Foaming, rushing tides
Swell and rise to highest peak,
Meet and greet
Golden moon;
Lunar glow magnetize ocean flows
In divine bliss.

Your expressions may be
Far more picturesque than mine,
Had you only time to share.
Close to the sea, away from the crowd.
It's a phase-can't wait.
A match made in heaven,
The wedding must go on.

Rolling, roaring, wailing,
Beautiful monster tides;
Like pageant making strides.

Delicate fragrance from the ocean floor,
Like short breaths of fresh spring air,
Warmed the atmosphere.
Miles of classical music,
Tidal songs.

Singing, laughing, groaning, mourning.
Reflection of life's changing moments.
Harder they came with crescendo,
So softly they fall.
Into the arms of anchored rocks
Aquatic grandeur defined,
I stood in awe!

Like the eve of Christmas,
Fantastic ballroom dance,
Humongous tides rise to celestial heights,
Hugged the flirting puffy clouds
Gently touched the golden sky,
Hopped, skipped, spun, and splashed.
Ripple waves spread all around,
Leaving their silver lining, lacey gowns.
Transforming into little bubbles
Changing colours.

Blue, green, pink, purple, orange, yellow.
Waves of beauties, darting-kissing bubbles,
How grown they seemed
In just a little while.
All in rhythmic motion,
Dancing to the beat
Sweet oceanic serenade.

Songs of Solomon
Taught me wisdom.
Easter cantata was solemn,
The Death of All Death.
Single Parent sonata filled my heart
With cheers.

I was deeply inspired
By lots of musical medleys.

Noble music resounding.
Mozart, The Requiem,
Beethoven, Moonlight Sonata.
Could not compare with Musical Tides.
Then I reminded myself,
Human beings are not perfect.
This is supernatural.

Like a curious child,
In the far distance I gazed.
There were no stars in the sky.
Among the tides they twinkled by.
Magnitude of exatic pictures in phases,
For the first moment,
I thought I had a peek in the Sistine Chapel.
Magnificent art displayed
Images of every nature,

At the blink of an eye,
They appeared and melted one into another.
Holy matrimony!
Each was unique,
Each was a masterpiece.

Again, I reminded myself,
Picasso, Rembrandt, Matisse.
Van Gough, DaVinci
Their finest,
I could never compare;
The Divine stands alone.
Glowing Tide is super natural.

Tears coursed my cheeks.
The fascination fed my soul;
Total rejuvenation,
A blissful euphoric relam.

Suddenly,
A friendly majestic sound
from the audience of
Clouds, mountains, trees and valleys.
The harmonious tone was all around ,
Above and beyond.

A soft whispering voice,
"My dear, you've seen nothing yet.
Imagine the tiny fauna and flora,
Boosting reproductive activity in pleasure.

Somethings are beyond human understanding.
Everything for my children fullfillment.

The ocean and mother earth are my laboratory,
Not a dark room.

Forget about all that my love,
Humankind are my most sacred creation.
Eyes have not seen,
Ears have not heard,
Precious fortune in store for my children.
The things you have seen are transient;
Things cannot be seen are eternal.
My love for you all is new every day."
If I am dreaming, let me dream on.

THE WORLD IS YOUR STAGE

Be yourself.
By yourself you are not alone.
The world is your stage.
It's a monologue or maybe
Pantomime.
Make a great impression,
Show off without a vain show.
It's not about the first prize.
Your best is good enough.

Tonight the world may be your audience.
Tomorrow, you the mirror.
Figure out -
Where, the world.
Characters: me, myself, and I, the critique.
Time of my life.

Love and loyalty within myself,
Hope, and faith I face.
My fort.
There may be a second chance,
It's okay to make mistakes,
Just not the same one twice.

A name to bear:
For my fellowmen,
Ancestors,
New generations
Hold the torch high.
Excellence is the name of the game.

It's a race,
The human race, a marathon
Meaningful strides,
Sprint.
Different pace, one race.
A relay.
Pass on the baton.
Leave invisible handprints on
Indelible hearts of fame.

LOVE YOUR HEART

Start fresh.
Create a healthy dish.
Fresh vegetables, chicken, fish,
Meat or beans, whatever you prefer.
Sometimes you just have to switch.
Consider Kosher or sea salt.
A teaspoon or less per day.
It has less sodium per teaspoon than regular.
Lower the salt, love your heart.

Roasting or grilling,
Bring out the natural sweetness.
Lower the salt, love your heart.

"Experiment with spices,
Ginger, lime, or grated lemon zest."
Top chef said,
"A variety of seasoning blends,
Fresh and dried herbs.
Balsamic vinegar, varieties of flavours,
Cherries and figs,
Bring out the great savour in a dish."
Lower the salt, love your heart.

African Americans, others at risk.
Just be sleek.
Lower the salt. Love your heart.

MY MUSIC

Music helps to lifts my feeling
When I am down.
I have a CD player,
Selection of music
For my very own.
Boom box stick.

Different genres and artists,
Some from foreign lands.
Find the country on the map
Match with every song.
Do my chores to a soundtrack
Mom and I select.
Boom box stick

Sometimes she just shook her head
And laughed at me.
Other times we sing,
Laughed, and danced.
We enjoy that special bond.
Boom box stick.

Create my own special song,
Acapella, sing a lullaby.

Rap a bedtime story,
Bang my spoon on boxes, walls,
Or anything that looks right.
Boom box stick.

Rhythmic beat just like a drum.
I can't help but dance.
Mom is my number one fan.
"In everything, give thanks."
Boom box stick.

WHEN THE DAY RISES

New day,
You and me with songs.
Heavy bass echo, when
I tremble the strings of an old, old guitar.
Rhythm and sensation emerge.
I lean on a huge rock,
Like a tower, higher than I.
You'll see when the day rise.
Just me,
Different beats through the heat of the day.
Take your seat.
Do not try to compete.
Divine meditation,
When this new day rises.

Speak with me, diary of the heart,
Display your fine arts.
I request new songs each day.
Spring sweet conscious lyrics;
Like an oasis,
Refresh my soul.
Let me sing cool songs,
When today rises.

Words will flow like a river.
Spontaneous,
Courageous,
Inspiring.
The world keeps on turning,
New songs emerging,
Straight from the heart.

Joy found in precious moments.
Sweet melodies
Here and now.
Not tomorrow
When today rises.

PORTRAIT OF AN ARTIST

This day I shall do a portrait of the artist.
One of beauty, poise, and fame.
Contrast of colours will glow from an angle
Adorned with golden picturesque frame.
Even at nights it will shine.
All those who looked upon
Will stand back in awe!
A masterpiece.

I will carefully choose colours and style,
Delicate mixtures of paint,
Smoothest contour brushes,
Canvas of finest grain.
With patience and pride, every last stroke
Evoked joy and grace,
Like the winner of the Pulitzer Prize.

Portrait of my youth
Could have done decades ago,
Never a thought.
Assignments: Spain, Africa, Jamaica, and back.
Paintings I've made for men of much valour,
Mayors, majesties, presidents,
Million and billionaires,

Royalties from everywhere.
Doing my own should be much easier than theirs,
Plus my years of expertise.

It shall be bold, beautiful, and free,
Eyes that sparkle, and contour cheeks,
Rosy lips reflecting love.
Graceful demure; character impart.
Portrait of an artist, "The Great."

Composure illuminated like the rising sun,
Blissful inspiration,
Historical beauty slide on digital screen,
Precious memories unfolded.

Savour the time,
A cup of warm tea,
News from countries I don't even know.
Burnt toast didn't taste too bad today.
Nothing shall take from my happy, happy nest.

Oh, my special art.
Beautiful day.

Ah,
What's bugging me now?
In my mind's eye,

I saw you, and,
Many others I don't even recognize.
Why?

I questioned my mind,
For hours
I wrestled with my heart and soul,
Why am I having second thoughts,
I finally came to realize,
The content of the art
I'm about to start,
It's all about a famous artist
"Me."

How vainly I boasted of beauty,
Skill and success.
A portrait of myself,
The perfect silhouette

Oh, no! Portrait of myself
I'll never paint on canvas,
Not with the finest stroke of brush, or,
Time I have to waste.

The real portrait is you,
The teachers who go above and beyond
To help their students understand.

The postman who never open someone's mail.

Those who never littered the streets.
Workers that helped their companies grow.
Citizens who brought
Fundamental issues to awareness.

You are the
Real portrait of an artist.

The young man who found the lost child
And brought her back home safely,
He is a national symbol.

All are bold and beautiful,
You sparkle.
The contents of your character,
Your love for humanity,
Makes you
The perfect silhouette.
You are my portrait.

IN MY HEART

Tribute to my husband
(The late)
Rev. Winston J. Pledger.

In my heart you'll always be
A love that was so dear,
A Purple Heart and folded flag
Reflect your love for humanity.
There is one who loves you more,
Cares for you much more than me.

Love forever.

FORECLOSURE, YOU MONSTER (PART TWO)

Foreclosure, monster hopping,
Free loading.
Try to rob me of my housing;
Like my cheating husband, Lova,
No one can take him!
I stood up strong!
When Bulletta tried to steal him.
Let lay low,
For a lousy bank to take my house.
No way!

This is my only home sweet home.
I am not going down, down, down.

No prejudice in taking risk.
Lots of scenario,
Plans to ring in more dinero.

Have a yard sale.
Do a bake sale,
Fish-cake, cookies, real ginger ale.

Go low on cold cereal,
I love hot porridge.

Got to build up my courage,
To pay up the mortgage.

If I have to work from four to four
I must hang on the keys to my door

In this dilemma.
I have to be a winner.
Cultivate some flowers,
Different colours.
Earn fistful of dollars.

Make wedding bouquets,
Host baby shower,
Enter flower shows,
Sell to those on the go.
Christmas, Valentine, Easter fest,
No rest till I clear the mess.

Step up to the table,
Cut down on the cable.

Decorate my garage,
Host comedy show, entitled,
"Together, All."
Invite parents, friends and teens.
Pantomime the queen of means.
And other interesting scenes.

Help bring joy in our little community,
There is no entertainment in this area.
My garage will be your oasis.
Please make sure you leave some dough
Before you go.

Parents coming home late from work,
"Keep children safe" is my pet project.
Life's science is the way to go—
They'll learn how a garden grow
From week to week,
Hands on planting seeds and sprigs.
See cucumber tendrils climb the fence.
Tomatoes and potatoes upside down.
Fruit of the loom is not underwear.

Treats they will learn to share.
Saige Antoine won't be sitting on the phone.
Sheila and Keylan skip to the loop in my rope.
Scott and Keira dance hoola hoop.

Lots of fun in store for them,
Gazing at backyard birds and animals
One red rooster rules the roost,
All hens reproduce.
Don't count the eggs before they hatch.
Can't give chicken corn to carry.
Don't put all your eggs in the same basket.

A bird in the hand worth two in the bush.
Chicken running around with its head cut off.
Why did the chicken cross the street?

They will know why
The mouse ran up the clock.
The cat fiddles around
While the little dog laughs;
Puss playing with the bone,
While dog wants it.
Close the gate before the horse comes out.
Carry the horse to the water,
But can't force it to drink.
Don't put pearls in the mouth of swine.
See a brown cow eats fresh green grass
And give sweet white milk.
Holy cow!

The goal is to learn, earn and inspire,
Only a poor rat has but one hole.
Don't tell that to my lova.

Major debts are out the way.
I can now save for rainy day,
In the comfort of my home.

THE BEST GIFT OF ALL

Beautiful bouquet of roses,
Basket with delicious fruits,
The islands or ocean cruise,
Gift certificates to our favourite stores,
We come full circle with gifts we can share;
Great are these gift, comfort divine.

Family members,
God, parents, and friends,
The only time we spend together
As a cheerful group, are times like:
Reunions, birthday parties, weddings.
Time together, profoundly cherished,
The best gift of all.

We the children are the future,
Family's pride and joy.
From the oldest to the youngest
Family member,
All are shining stars.

Grand parents, like parents,
Are special.
Nothing comes between us.

Always adore
How much we have grown.
"Com'on baby," their awesome request,
Give Nana some sugar, Kissy, kissy, kiss."

We are always their babies,
No matter how much we have grown.
They not only showed interest in us,
But also our friends.
Giving their blessings on the goals that we seek.

A special place in our hearts,
Loving aunts, uncles, and cousins,
Their warm embrace.
Just the thought of them set our hearts aglow.

God mother and God father,
Another name for angels.
They keep up with us.
Make sure we do the right thing.
Know just when to pop in or call.

Time, the glue that binds our love,
Precious memories,
Best gift of all.

SAFER ZONE

The Queen of talk shines a bright light,
Recommends
Make the USA a safer place,
No phone zone.

No phone call, no texting while driving.
Take the pledge.
No phone zone.

Gone beyond the USA,
Foreign lands-back a yard.
Everyone is a neighbour,
Family, or friend.

Tell them nicely,
"If I call while you are driving,
Pull over at a safe spot, or,
Wait till you get home."
No phone zone is everywhere.

We travel on business,
We travel for pleasure.
It should be safe, wherever we go.
No phone zone is everywhere.

Stick to the pledge like potent glue.
No one should make a stupid mistake,
Living with deadly guilt for the rest of your life.
"If I did know, it is left behind the door."
Cannot turn back the hands of time.

Driving while texting or talking,
Is just as irresponsible as
Sleeping behind the wheels,
Or drunk and drive.

I don't want to see you cry
Don't want to hear no one died
Hate to say goodbye.
Smile.
Save your life, our loved ones too.
Drive, ride, and walk with care.
No phone zone is everywhere.

HAPPY FACE

Patricka Daley-Pledger

A happy face is one of grace.
Some things just make me smile.
Flowers, babies, music, fruits,
Delicious dishes.
Whoever picks me up from school.

If I meet someone I admire,
We share a soft smile.
Wrapping gifts for friends and family,
When I give to charity,
I can't help but smile.

Making pastries is so much fun,
I am tempted to

Lick the sweet-smelling batter from the bowl,
That just makes me smile.
Story time, Easter egg hunt,
Sharing happy times.

A big smile is on me,
When I see my family enjoying a nice meal;
Especially that which I helped to prepare.
Happy face is like greeting the sunrise.

LIKE IT IS

In every situation,
You need a good education,
Need a skill,
Strong will, to earn your way through life.
You won't forever be
Mommy's little one or
Daddy's little one.

When we are gone from here,
You will be on your own.
Maybe have a family.
There may be little people in your life,
Look just like you.
You will have to make decisions,
Just like Dad,
Keep the family together,
Just like Mom.
Have responsibilities, morality,
Be a role model.
Nurture them right.
Some day they will be just like you.

IMAGINE TOMORROW

What would it take to make you happier,
If it would all come through
Imagine tomorrow.
Would it be,
Winning the lottery,
Fantasy-filled,
Un-break your heart?

Imagine tomorrow.
I'd be happier if the world we are a part of
Strove for:
Respect, truth, and justice,
Peace, love, honesty,
Faith, self-determination,
Work and responsibilities.

Imagine our tomorrow
For the world to be a better place,
Leaving it more beautiful, safe, and beneficial
For others to inherit.

THE PASSAGE OF TIME

I used to skip down the road,
Hold hands with my friends,
Hopes to achieve every new day.
School was safe, fun was fun,
Milk, eggs, used to be cheap,
Times were good,
I remember when ...
Those were,
Some of my good old days.
The passage of time.

It is still a beautiful world.
Things have changed,
Some things will always remain the same.
Native species are fewer,
Some are on the brink of extinction.
Global warming is on the rise,
It will impact the future.
Eco friendly is great world investment,
Each of us can make a difference;
Recycle, go green,
Plant more trees.

Modern technology,

Continue to magnify fast-paced nations.
The computer phenomenon,
Absolutely an evolution revolution.

There is something good in,
Many things that you will see.
It will always be,
Wonderful world with beautiful people.
These will be your "good old days."
Make it better for the next generation
Through the passage of time.

MY SPECIAL WORLD

My special world,
A positive state of mind.
Levels of happiness depends on me.
Sharp focus on appearance,
Maintain sanity.

My special world is flavoured with:
Families, friends, acquaintances,
Fans and well wishers.
In fact everyone.

My special world is coloured with
Empowerment,
Ambition,
Curiosity,
Discipline and diligence,
Innovation,
Leap of faith.

I am not offended by negative criticism,
But instead learn from them.
Obstacles are my stepping stones.
I motivate myself to get things done,
I am a new person every day.

My special world, concern for all.
Prayers for the end of war;
All men shall live in peace.
Faith and wisdom for our leaders.
Strength to stand firm for the weak.
Love for one another.

LONGEVITY

The great gift of life
Live to be close to a century or more,
Continue to give praise and glorify,
Have great appreciation for life.
It will be okay when
Succumbing heart gives in.
Give credit to healthy living, honesty,
Love for animals, and humanity.

I am no legend,
Just a living history book,
I demand no folly, full respect for my rights.
The grandchildren and great-grandchildren,
Are stars in my crown.

Turning point, eat to live.
Body is weaker, spirit gets brighter.
Great admiration when they dress me.
Take me wherever they want me to go.
Expect nothing but love and gratitude.
The journey,
A long path, paved with good and bad.
It was not always a bed of roses,
But granted much wisdom.

Memories faded over the years,
Like the shadow of a rainbow.
Video images remained strong,
Vivid, just like yesterday,
Played out, like classic movies.

Matters not how long I shall live,
Happy I will be.
The seeds I have sowed,
That's what I'll reap.

DARE NOT COMPARE

I am grateful for what I have.
I am not sad or mad if,
Someone at work
Make more money than I,
Or, other students get better grades.
If some one has a nice car, clothes
Or anything else,
I'd just be happy for them.
And be content.
Dare not compare.

Some subjects are
Just not my favourite.
But if my grades are not up to par
I will certainly raise the bar.
Take a deeper dive in my books
And at the library.
Stay up later,
Study harder, ask for help.
Advance my grades a notch or two.

1,2 don't want you.
3, 4 want more.
5, 6, 7, 8 up the ladder,
9, 10, a big fat A plus.
This is the only time I compare.

DIFFERENCE EMBRACE

In my eyes you are who you are.
I dare not see you as:
Fat, skinny, gay straight, black or white
Everyone is a friend.

It would be inappropriate to label you by:
Colour, creed, physical statue, religion,
Or sexual orientation.

Gossip about you.
Verbally attacking you.
What would be my motive?
Do I hope to accomplish anything,
Other than attracting negative
attention to myself.

Your appearance and
Your personality is no one's business.

It is obvious, we are
More alike than different.
We make our contribution to society,
Breathe the same air,
Have the capacity to love

Everyone's blood is red.
The same sun shines for you
Shines for me
Instead of taking matters in our own hands,
Leave it alone, in the master's hand.

Show respect instead of
Anger and sarcasm.
We cannot change people
But we can certainly portray good attitude.
Ask for courage to embrace the difference.
Like the colours of the rainbow,
We are connected by one magnificent bond.

I'd rather work along with an
honest, industrious gay;
Than with a lazy, crooked, straight.
Difference embrace.

HEARTS IN THE PAST

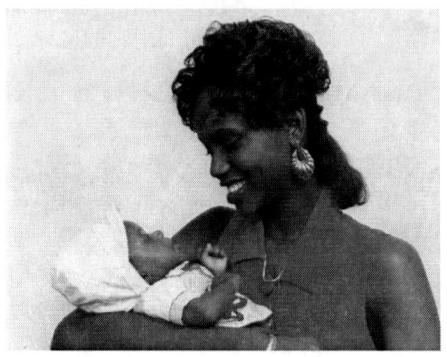

A soft, silent kiss on my cheek,
Just like the beautiful morning before.
A package message conveyed,
"Good morning
Love you; see you later."
Sealed with a another tender kiss,
Another and another.

I did not open my eyes,
Nor did I reply,
Just turned on the other side.
Though it's the third trimester,

Morning sickness sometimes takes a toll.
Even while I dream.

A sloppy kiss,
Obo, our miniature poodle.
We both enjoyed the first meal of the day.
I scooped up what seemed like dust,
Rushed to the foyer, reached over
To the aquarium.

Thum-Thum did not shoot up.
Did not feel the piercing snap on my fingers,
Like all the other times.
It was lying motionless in the jar.
I panicked a little,
Then said a prayer.

I watched it
Swept away by the torrid current.
Hoping its spirit would ascend a spiritual realm
Where all dogs go.
It was Tuesday, September 11, 2001.
Shortly before 9:00 a.m. the phone rang.

"Honey, a plane just hit tower one,
Think that's a commercial,
But we are evacuating."

I looked through my window
The second tower was now engulfed
My world seemed to stop turning.

In awe, I watched,
The massive tower came tumbling down.
Never would I see you again.
I whispered.
"Never feel your loving arms around me,
Tonight."
I knew it. I cried.

What about our unborn child?
We had already chosen a name.
I sobbed,
You can't leave!
It's a joy to watch children grow.
Every child needs a father. You can't go.
We need you. I love you.
I watched it over and over again on TV.

Then watched it in my mind's eye.
Family, friends, and neighbours,
Arrived one by one.
Some I did not recognize.
They wept; I mourned.

Every day,
Seemed to be the same without him.

A secret hope that he would still be alive.
DNA result matched remains recovered.
Memorial service,
Outpouring support continued.
The pianist solemnly played,
"Guide Me O Thou Great Jehovah."
I reminisced the time we first met.

The clock on the wall,
Constant reminder,
The time he would be home.
I listened for the key in the door,
My days were unsteady.
I knew I had to accept,
Like so many others.

I Visited ground zero;
It brought me little comfort.
Once used to be too busy, now,
Smoking rubbles.
How could anyone survive?
I said in laughingly words.
"Death cannot feel the past."

I then realized how fragile life really is,
Here this hour, gone the next.

When it seemed like all was gone.
Joy in the midst of pain.
Overwhelmed!
Bundle of joy rests between my breasts.
He should have been here,
Enjoying the bliss of birth,
Holding me, I said to myself.

Never did I miss him so much.
A tear, then
Smiles as I gazed at our son,
This moment a life has began.
I focused on my son's future,
Mummy's new man.
He will sleep on Daddy's side of the bed.
For him I'll give my last breath.
Thoughts of my husband in my heart.
Junior will always be
In the comfort of my arms.
9.11.2001. Remembered.

LETTER TO MY DAUGHTER

As you journey the path of success,
My wish for you,
Wisdom, knowledge and understanding.
Take life in humble strides
Each day as it glides.

Have time for others,
Speak less, listen more,
Try to see the other side.
"Truth has no sides."
Be forgiving no matter what.

With caution,
Expose a problem to the right source,
Instead of covering under the rug,
Decent exposure.
Let friends feel better when
They hang up the phone,
Or, when they leave.

Your faith and determination
Make difficult ordeals,
Seem funny and effortless.
Take time and smell the flowers.

Your accomplishment is Mom's gift,
Stand firm while your heart soars.
God bless.

Pass it on to others.
My love, timeless.

CELEBRATE

Life is full of unique moments,
Commemorate and cherish,
Flame of humanity keeps on burning.
Celebrate

Birthdays, anniversaries,
Your special day of the year,
An accomplishment,
Something meaningful,
A problem solved.
Celebrate the world and all its beauty.

While we celebrate,
Enjoy the music, delicious dishes.
Reasons to celebrate the season.
Keep friendship alive!

Celebrate life:
Those who survive an illness,
Remembering,
Those who did not make it.
Celebrate,
Any event with purpose and grace.
Acknowledge,
The bond of great relationship.

FACE TO THE VOICE

Revered and adored everywhere.
Unique and recognizable voice.
First name is of much fame.
Reversed the spelling,
It's still a shining flame.
Blessed,
Extraordinary strength and talents.

Overcome many obstacles
Faced challenges,
Broke strong barriers,
Many generations come to know her,
Covered many issues in her talk show.
Inspired us to do great things.

A chapter closed, not the whole book.
Shows in diversity, *OWN*
Provided moral support for many families,
Brought joy in the lives of others.
A humble being,
Regardless of fame and fortune.
She is loved and beloved.

Graced the covers of countless magazines.
Reached the level of success
Many only dreamed of.
A breath of fresh air.
Has an xtraordinary sense of humour.

Pop-culture icon,
In touch with the times,
A symbol of hope.
Some called her role model,
Others named her icon,
Queen of talk show.
They say friend.

Her children in Africa call her, "Mother"
*O*asis
*P*hilanthropist
*R*adiant
*A*dored
*H*eroine.

HELLO, GRADUATES

Like a butterfly,
You blossomed beautifully.
Make the world a brighter and better place.
Sometimes you may stumble and fall.
Each time you'll rise stronger than before.

Overcoming
Obstacles that seemed to hinder your path,
No matter how small or impossibly grand,
Experience gained,
Each time more profound.

Icons made tremendous impact in their time,
A journey, many have followed.

Their footprints you may trace;
Blend well with ambition.

Keep on discovering ways to unlock your potential,
New path you'll carve.
They will see your shining light,
Even from a distance.

Leave footprints!

GRADUATES, FRIENDS, AND FAMILY

It's here again,
Graduation in the air!
The wonderment of spring.
Out of the heavy winter coat;
Into modestly-sexy-spring-outfits.
Plants returning from the earth
Welcoming a new season,
All life reflecting spring.
Graduation Day!

Magnificent blooms,
Bright red and yellow bird of paradise,
Dove-white magnolias,
Roses, and apple blossoms,
Fragrantly sweetened the air.
Graduation Day!

The buzzing bumble bees and,
Melodious chirping of feathered friends
Ushered us beautifully, into,
Uplifting adoration ceremony.
Graduation Day!

Significant essence, claiming,
Accomplishment,
Feel the strong graduation vibes.
Dreams conceived, thoughts perceived
Opportunities pursued, everyone succeeded.
Graduation Day!

Don't cry, don't cry, don't cry.
It certainly paid off.
Rise at the crack of dawn; rain, snow, or shine,
Some days without lunch.
Committed students beat the odds.
Graduation Day!

Reaching for the sky.
If they miss, the stars they will hit.
Friends and families travelled near and far.
They joyously shared the pride.
Graduation Day!

Graduates saluted,
Faithfully supported, and adored.
Younger boys and girls have a
glimpse of their future.
They peered at graduates and
Imagine their future.
Older folks are reminded how they used to be
And feel tickled.

Graduation Day!

All dressed up or down, glamorous hairdos,
Fashion and styles, the latest and best,
Grace portrayed,
Everyone is number one.
Embrace something big.
Excitement!
Five years old, or over fifty,
It doesn't matter, important milestone reached.
Graduation Day!

Chocolate and bouquets await.
Graduates alive! along the aisles.
Stretch-forth for a certificate,
The key that will open many doors, their world
Everyone seemed to be daintily escorted by,
Heavenly angels.
Oh ya, angels are here too,
God is in this,
It's a heavenly dream come through.
Graduation Day!

Under the sky, rain or shine.
Friends and families stood tall,
Thank goodness! a great view.
I tried not to blink or wink my eyes.
Didn't want to miss one innocent smile,

Graduation Day!

It was like a sweet dream I didn't want to end.
Excellent speeches.
"Graduates work has just began.
Their faces to the future, hands on the wheel.
Keep it turning."
Graduation Day!

I prayed that,
They will be strong,
Their lives will always be seasons of spring.
May their dreams and wishes have wings.
I saw it in their eyes and,
I saw it in their smiles.
Graduation Day!

Party in honour of great success,
Staff, graduates, families and friends,
Want to have fun!
It's going to be a good day, into-the-night.
They are going to have a ball.
Graduation Day!

Strike a pose; say cheese! Family with grad,
Graduate with friends,
Solo.
Never realise how good a thing is,
Till you got it in your hand.

Graduation Day!

Party just began.
Rhythm sensation, steel bond alive.
Cool music will reach climatic vibes,
Calypso, classic, rap, cool reggae,
Lyrics dedicated to everyone.
Graduation Day!

People like sand, clapping hands.
Body-rock, body-move, springy feet.
Love to give, life to live.
Sweet hours, day into-night,
Graduation Day!

I looked around and they were gone.
Mother kept them all, in my prayers.
Memories remained.
Long remembered,
Congratulations, class of _ _ _ _.

LEAVE A BETTER PLANET

Deep Well Horizon exploded,
killed *B*eyond *P*eople,
Everything above, around, and *B*elow *P*lateau.
Catastrophe *B*eyond *P*reposterous.
Tar ball adhered to sea food, *B*irds and *P*lants,
They could not predict the spill,
*B*efore oil *P*ressure rises
Would have sealed the *B*looming *P*lug.
Continuous spewing of *B*lack
*P*ollution into the gulf.

*B*eastly *P*redators! *B*lack *P*hantom!
Devastation to *B*rother *P*arker and everyone else,
They lost *B*oats and *P*artnerships.
That was a *B*ig *P*art of his investment.
Let us *B*ring *P*eace back to their lives?
And *B*uild *P*rogressive communities?
*B*eyond *P*leasure!

SEE THE LIGHT

Wake up, wake up!
See the light.
Wake up and get it together.
You'll be alright.

See the light at the end of the tunnel
It's not the oncoming train
That light is shining for you
A ray of hope.

Shake off, shake off!
Hate, fear, doubt and anger.
Put aside deeds of darkness.
Sow seeds of kindness.
Joy, peace, and love.

Clean up, dress up,
Know who you are,
Where you are.
Be a strong rock,
Leave what's holding you back.

Glow! Glow in the dark.
Walk in the sunshine, skip the rain.

Read, sing, you can't be silent.
Do something, before something do you.
You could be the one driving the train,
The face behind the light in the tunnel.
Fallow your renewed heart.

OVERCOMING GRIEF

Anyone who has experienced the loss of a loved one,
Knows the kind of pain that never
completely subsides.
As human we are susceptible to
various kinds of weaknesses,
Such as loneliness and depression.
It was not long after my husband passed,
These feelings became evident.
I decided to do something constructive,
By designing a garden,

The sweet beginning of spring,
Lifted my spirit.
My imagination,
Leaped beyond description
As I communed with my subjects.
I carefully chose a spot,
Dug soil, and transferred water from a well.
Fondly I gazed over the sunset mountain.
Interesting thoughts refreshed my soul.
I felt love in the heart of nature.

Whistling spring breeze,
Blue sky, fluffy clouds shuffling by.

Soil as old as Mother Earth.
Water from a well that
Holds the secret of its sources.
Living plants, birds and insect,
Offspring like you and me,
A new flower garden.
"All things bright and beautiful."
I rejoiced.

A smart black-and-white Labrador retriever,
Became the second member of my household.
Smooth bonding in no time,
I realized that he was the one that chose me,
Not me choosing him.

My sister named him Rocky.
Since then, there is never a dull moment.
I feel so delighted when he welcomes me home.
He remains a blessing in my life.

Tending to the garden,
Caring for my dog,
Giving that special care,
I interact with the natural values of life.
It gives a sense of fulfilment,
Everything in life has a greater value and purpose.

INDELIBLE IMAGES

Events, incidents,
People, places, and things.
Perceptions
Captivate the impressive,
Fully aware or subconscious.
Bitter, sweet,
Deeply moving experiences,
Images resonate.
Disappearing factors,
Remaining chapters,
Indelible images stand the test of time.

Pain, love, happiness, laughter.
Supreme judgment in time, take effect,
Subjects to let go, and those to grasp.
"We journey with the memories,
We cannot erase."

House made of straw,
The wind blew away;
Those made of wood,
Stood for a good while;
Gifts for tender hearts to keep,
Like a house made of brick;

Stand strong.
No degree of separation.
Indelible images.

Precious memories empowered,
The acts that made us cringe.
Birth, baptismal, wedding, a visit.
Memories sparkle from our hearts.
This may be the right time,
Give someone "Dear" a call.

Dark clouds may try to steal across,
Where the tempest seemed low.
Vibrant, indelible images stand firm with you.
Fun memories come alive!
Impossible to contain.
Reflecting grace like the portrait of someone,
You love,
Those who care.
Indelible images.

MY WEB AND TV SAVVY PARENTS

I admire everything about my
Web and TV savvy parents.
Mom and Dad model the behaviour
They would like us to have.

They chose the shows that
Matched our family values.
Entertained only what's appropriate.
Programs that encouraged
Kindness, respect, and self-esteem.
Lessons about caring and sharing,
Resolving disagreement.

Like good parents and teachers,
Web, TV, and family magazine
Send positive messages to us.
We learn more about our world,
Good source of
Education and entertainment.

Our home training
Strongly influence our lives;
In their absence

We never stray from their upbringing.
I enjoy a balance life.

Our home, our haven.
Web and TV savvy parents.

FLOWERS WITHOUT BORDERS

Flowers,
Colourful, cheerful giving.
Nature's way, saying
"Hi! Hello! Cheers!
Congratulation."
Extending peace, welcome home.
Love, greet, grief, reconcile.
Inexpressible gift.

Need no wrapping with a bow,
Always appropriate for the go,
Plenty at the flower show,
Set our hearts aglow.

Flowers,
Make the dark days bright,
Such a delight.
Place them on shelves,
Indulge yourselves
Desks, countertops, windowsill.
Plant them along walkways,
Highways, and driveways.
Gracefully adorn outside and in,
Hospitals, homes, school.

Beautiful girls,
Clover, Rose, and Hyacinth,
Like to wear flowers in their hair.
Bouquets hold tight before she says
"I do."
The next bride-to-be will catch with
Joy.

Let's celebrate!
My friend in England is about
To give birth, bundle of joy!
Proud parents welcome
Beautiful bouquets.
Cheerful giving.

Loved ones
Celebrating birthday,
Trinidad, Africa, Canada.
Flowers on the go!
Take some home
For the family to enjoy.
Flowers without borders.

"Roses are red, violets are blue,
Sugar is sweet,
But not as sweet as you."

Flowers, centrepiece of the world.
Flowers fade,
But God's words stand forever.

ONE WHITE GLOVE

Shed no more tears of love,
Precious loved ones will carry on.
Sparkle, sparkle little stars.
They will glow like my white glove.
Prince and princess will shelter blanket;
They are my jewels.

Wrapped in our family's
Warm and tender love,
Treasure money can't buy.
I will be there when they need me.
Hear and feel me in my music.
I am your shadow.
Dance, let the music play.

Adoring fans asked, "Why?"
Hold on to the sovereign's hand.
Divine guidance; never, never let go.
Never say good-bye.

One white glove
Symbolizes peace and love.
All good things from the Father above.
Love and affection

Gives me spiritual satisfaction.
"We are the world"; we are his people.
Pope and pauper.
All children of the awesome God.

One glowing white glove,
Significance of a unique man
Reflections of my music
Here to eternity.
"Black And White, Heal The World"

Representation of my dynasty
One of a kind. Neverland.

Glowing white glove,
Like sun shining through the rain.
Had my share of trials and pain;
Tripled success and gain.
The king of pop rocks.
The man, the music, the mirror.
I will reflect brighter than yesteryears
All negativity will certainly disappear.

One glove, why not a pair?
Like the peaceful white dove
With the olive branch,
Link a bond to my soul.

God of the children, you are my master.
I am lost. Will you find me?

Take me!
"Carry me like you are my brother,
Hold me softly and boldly."
Take me across
Rivers of diamond and mountains of gold.
"Softly then boldly, carry me there."

Hold my hand.
Lead me,
Lead me to the promise land.

RESPECT

Respect is due to everyone,
No matter how young, or how old.
Respect for one and all
Regardless of
Gender, race, colour, or creed.

Give respect by not
Instigating confrontation,
Infuriating frustration to the
Point of desperation,
Escalating negativity.

Do not say or write words
In public places that hurt others.
Never make others the "end" of your joke.

Let's live in peace, love, and unity.
Not everyone is calm, cool,
And collected like you and me.
The life you save could be your own.

BUCKLE UP

Buckle up, buckle up!
It's the law.
Buckle up baby for your own safety.
Men, women, boys, and girls.
Slide it cross your shoulder,
Click it in the buckle.

Love your seatbelt
Like
You love somebody.
It hugs and protect.

Buckle up babies in car seats.
Taller babies, booster seats.
Check out your state laws.
They all agreed on one thing.
"Buckle up."

No matter if you're going
Just round the corner,
Or if you are going
All the way past Long Acre.
Buckle up babies,
Their lives depend on you.

Patricka Daley-Pledger

Love your seat belt,
Like,
You love somebody.
It hugs and protect.

Buckle up. It's the law.

INTERNET SPIDERS

Itsy, bitsy spiders,
Tarantellas, and black widows,
We copied your webs and made it ours.
You should have had it patented,
This may never happen.

You were the first I know to
Build fantastic webs,
Sites on fences, branches,
In the corners of my room.
Magnificent networking.

You logged on, surfed, devoured your prey,
But that's your nature.

Some genius unlocked the "gate";
Ideas spiralled across the globe.
Social networking, corporate networking
Were made with good intent.

Internet spiders deploy clever devices,
Corrupt the system.
With sweet talks and false promises,
They made our children prey.

Predators! Refrain from cyber:
Pervert-ism, fraud, bullying,
Espionage and warfare.
That's not your true nature,
Shame on you!

Beware of the "Black Widows";
They were never married.

DEAR MOM AND DAD

Hope you had a great vacation.
I can imagine how surprised you were
To see my bed neatly spread,
and clothes out of sight.
Please find the courage to read
this letter in its entirety.
Just to let you know that college
is no longer a priority.
My grades were failing anyway.
You always complain that,
All I do is eat, sleep, repeat

I met a man about twice my age.
He is as sweet as you can imagine.
He asked me to move in with him.
I told him it was not a problem.
I am bonding nicely with the kids,
Leslie, Jaygon, Dwight, and baby Josh.
They say that I am like an older sister.
It's not easy keeping up with them.
No time to eat, sleep, repeat.

It's not so bad; some of the mothers live nearby,
They dropped by to help out.

Wayne and I are trying to make ends meet.
I informed him of the scientific breakthrough
For his treatment.
I will make sure he take advantage of it.
He said that I am a port in a storm and that,
I give him and the children hope.

Next week he will start his drug rehab.
We hope to stop by so you can meet him.
You may not like his dread locks.
He says I will soon get used to it.
Please, can I have my bed please?

Stop! Hush. Take a deep breath.
This is a prank.
Just so that you would understand,
There are a lot of issues much more
Than my failing grades.

Don't worry.
I am surrounded with my books,
Studying hard in the attic.
College is my definite goal.
I'm tired of failing, failing, failing.
When you calm down,
"Knock three times on the ceiling
If you want me."

I have no time to eat, sleep, repeat.
Love and kisses
Repeater.
P.S. What's in a name?

THE PHOENIX

Lived my span of years beyond measured,
Every moment were not all treasured.
Now the weary body seeks eternal rest.
To die I must, but I will resist the test.

Within the pile, grey ash,
Slowly hushed my old body to death.
To die I must, to start anew.
But sure, I shall rise to the test.

Precious remains that was once graceful feathers.
Lie motionless, mere traces of tender ash.
Within the warm mound, like uterus
A heart of will slowly, silently, beating.

All is gone but the pulse hang on,
Patiently beating.
Like fetus, yearned for life,
A heart slowly, silently beating.

Brave soldiers do; I too shall fight.
Victory will be mine.
I will not yield to dim cremation;
There is great joy in restoration.

Flutter! flutter! Wings of gold.

You were once so bold.
Oh air! Sweet air!
Breathe me wind for my feeble wings.

Sigh on me, let me live. I have much to give.
Air! Oh air!
Unfold your strong arms and release your power.
Not like thunders of showers;
As dew-drops fall on summer's thirsty grass.

Shoo, gentle wind, slowly and softly.
I'm just fragile ash.
Cuddled within is a heart that's bold.
Air, pleasant fragrance rapture me.

Wind under my wings,
Spread them wide like a fan
Fan! Fan!–Fan wings fan.
You can do it! Yes you can!
Life! Oh life,
Capture me, the essence of my being.

Remind me how I use to be,
Strong, courageous and free.
You soared me high above the clouds.
The awesome universe we explored.

Parade of beauty adorned the sky.
Sweet melodies lingered as I fly.

When I returned to former glory,
Promised I will tell the story.

Blood in my vein roared with zest.
The will to live I possess.
I will truly confess,
This is an audacious request.

Gracefully from the sacred ground I rise.
Shimmering like a crystal chandelier.
Living, fluffy ball of purple-crimson feathers.
Beauty beyond compare.

I wonder.

Mid-air fluttering, flapping, flying-dancing.
Momentum rise higher, with each passing phase.
Clover, Sun bird, Cockatiel and
Humming bird,
Hushed their cry
With curiosity, from limb to limb
They floated closer and closer.
Then zoomed right in, happy jubilee!

I can fly, I can fly! I will fly away.
I am stronger and wiser,

The Phoenix never dies.
I am the Phoenix.

LOVE IS

Love is a crown, worn by everyone.
Love is without obsession.
It is not possessive.
Love is warm and tender
Love is all the answers,
Impart in the questions

Love is a treasure,
It cannot be measured.
Transcend any gender.
Love is a diamond,
It sparkles in everyone.
Love is like a little flower,
It has great power.

Love is old, but yet, new every day.
Love is you.

Patricka Daley-Pledger

MUSICAL ROSE

It has been a while since you've been gone.
We think about you night and day.
We admired your sensational energy.
Like a Terminator, creating momentum,
Dominating your guitar.

Singing, rocking, dancing across
world-wide stages.
You are a musical rose, in our
sacred garden grows.
Pioneered a dynasty of reggae
music across the world.

Help to gained global recognition
for our precious island.
"Jamaica! Jamaica, land we love."

Legend of all times; "Brother of wisdom."
Sing loud your songs of time.
"Awake to reality, the evolution sleepers."

We hear your voice in every reggae beat.
Inspired every new generation; all nation.
Promote peace, love, understanding
in lyrical vibes.
Reggae dance of universal spirit.
Your philosophy, our legacy.

Like magic played in our homes,
cars, mall, and dance hall.
Echoes in our hearts everywhere we go.
Charismatic reggae vibes.
Reminding us.

"Don't worry about a thing.
Cause,
Every little thing is going to be all right."

You conveyed positive messages to our souls.
If only we would listen,

Great lessons we could learn.
Let's play them on - on - on.

Maybe we can dance, dance.
Just dance till we feel the feelings.
Sweet, sweet reggae musical rose.

*B*rave
*O*lder
*B*rother

*M*usical
*A*rtist
*R*emembered
*L*egend
*E*ntertainer
*Y*ours.